blooming without notice

Jatelia Lewis

bloom: /bloōm/ (v.)

to mature. to transform and outgrow every hindrance and setback in your way. to grow and expand beautifully and gracefully.

Putting this book together awakened fear and tons of anxiety. For once, I am nearly giving anyone willing to open this book a look into eras of vulnerability and transparency. This is coming from someone who remained in the back and stayed quiet for the majority of her life (not that there has been much life lived). I was the epitome of the quiet black girl. Writing was all I had when speaking seemed to detest me. I questioned myself a lot, especially when it came to my writings. Sometimes I hated my craft and other times I was proud of it. It took me a while to even realize it was a craft. I prolonged releasing this as long as I could over the thought of myself being read. My motivation came from knowing there is at least one person on this earth who may appreciate my words. There could very well be someone who needs to read what I have to say. That always seemed so far-fetched to me.

I do not wish to be understood but I fancy to be heard. This book is only a small fragment of myself and my (incomplete) journey, but it is not all about me for the journey of others resonates with me, too. I have barely reached the surface of my twenties and my path is much longer. One day I decided to stop allowing my hurt and worries get too comfortable around me. From the relationship that I thought broke me to the toxic mindset I so heavily relied on, to the sufferings of others, every piece written in this book came from experiences, empathy and growth. I always said God does not give us ideas, visions and gifts to sleep on them. It was time for me to give the snooze button a rest. I have reached a place of comfort and resiliency; however, I am not perfect, and I have every right to feel and embrace whatever emotion crosses my path. You do, too.

blooming without notice covers three chapters simultaneously embodying phases of a flower to represent phases of personal growth. Many of the writings, prose and poetry were written before I even knew I would have a book, taken from personal journals I would never dare to share before. Chapter 1 is the wilting. This chapter features everything I have been afraid to discuss, or never felt comfortable doing so - depression, anxiety, heartbreak, self-hatred, doubt and the list goes on. Piecing each bit together was quite shameful at first, however, to look back at where I came from was refreshing. Chapter 2 is the pruning. Pruning is a process where the dead parts of plants are cut away to achieve better health, which in turn promotes growth. The cutting of the stem allows the plant to absorb more water, therefore reversing its wilting. As you could imagine, cutting things from your own life is required to move forward and reach desired goals. How ironic is it that we have to cut some things loose to become whole? The truth is there are things in our lives that need to be cut away because they offer no purpose, support stagnation and affect us negatively. When you are trying to get somewhere higher, everything cannot go with you.

This is the chapter of reflecting from what has been learned. This is the comeback.
The final chapter is the blooming. Blooming is about welcoming a new and improved person. When a flower blooms, it has gotten through tough seasons and has welcomed its growth to come into fruition. An individual blooming experiences a growth spurt of confidence, self-love, tranquility and all other possible good things one hopes to have. More importantly, blooming is about accepting and creating a home that welcomes your heart's desires. It is important to know that not even blossoming is a walk in the park, but now you realize your ability to withstand anything thrown your way to get you off track.

I hope this encourages you to embrace and love your journey of blossoming into the mesmerizing flower you are.

these are my words

raw

natural

and unapologetic

the wilting

lost, disoriented

and searching for answers

through the souls that gave me questions

a disservice.

defeat trapped me

behind doors created with no keys

exasperating.

salty, resentful water

consumed my face

like the darkness of thick smog

i naively walked through

looking for signs of any light,

of any life

grief.

you traded

soil

water

sunlight

for things already bloomed

but once you wilted

and your stem weakened

they had nothing to give

not like i did

- *lifeless*

i've attempted to force sleep

for the past six hours

to temporarily become unavailable to the

thoughts

and feels of the past twenty-four

to just simply forget.

i wrote and wrote then tossed

and tossed

to remove the despised feelings i am enduring

from my chest, limbs and every other part

where pain lingers

of my body where they've seemed to make a

home out of

and wave a white flag on occasion

that goes unnoticed

a relationship transpired
during this relationship
at your hands
at your will
and somehow you made sure that
i was made responsible
to mend this one

i am the switch you force on
to return to when needed
when lost
when others drift and
leave you in complete darkness

-   *don't ever try me again, 12/21/17*

i have sore eyes

from shedding the

works of you

-   *cleansing*

i am a magician, won't you believe

i appear in two places at once

i breathe and suffocate at the same time

i cry and smile in conversations, yet

you'll only witness one

i pray without opening my mouth

i hug while i use my arms to carry

loads of burdens not belonging to me

i yell 'i'm a mess' while whispering 'i'm fine'

and make sure you only hear the latter

i send affirmations to my mates

but forget myself sometimes

i left my heart in impure hands

on many occasions, yet

air still greets my lungs

sometimes i even write while i sleep at night

i wake at night

from the forbidden thoughts of

my mind

tossing and turning

restlessly

without even moving my body

wishing they could be calmed by

answers

- *constantly searching*

what will you tell God

after breaking the promises

made to Him

broken like the mirrors of my reflection

shattered, unfulfilled promises

of unconditional faithfulness

to His beloved child

what will you say

now that you have killed me

this knife of betrayal in my back

with great precision

slowly, gradually

paralyzing me

what will you say

now that you have stood over my lifeless body

waiting to say amen

like the man of faith falsely portrayed

what a saint

- *treachery*

i have to rush and

throw on my face

the one that they see

to cover up the one they don't

i wipe my tears and

put on clean clothes

to seem okay

and when they ask

"how are you?"

i will say

"great"

i can't recall the last time i was great

when your heart feels empty

but heavy

and your breaths are uneven

and your face feels tight

and your eyes are hungry

to be filled with light, again

or a spark at least

and you stare into space

searching for something

to make it right

to mend everything back together

to wait and not know

what you're waiting for

these are the hours

i will never forget

- *after hours*

i try too hard

to build up

and defend

what breaks me down

i would touch you and

swore it were someone else

where did you go, my love?

just as the intuition of my ancestors planted in me

are you hiding from me?

from us?

i sat across from your soul

my heart in my pockets so

it would not speak this time

and still i felt nothing

the house we built, vandalized

by burglars with keys and somehow

i still expected a home

that resembled cell blocks

to stand strong on my hands alone

weak foundations.

just as the mind i attracted

one day i'll be able

to think

without skipping breaths

there are not enough words

to calm the sea's current

of the uncontrollable medley

of my beating heart

coincided with the fears of revelation thrown

under rugs

dancing together as one

hands that shake tables of my future

involuntarily

grasp my trachea

to anticipate, or not

to save myself, or not

- *anxious*

if only you knew

the very thing that gave you life

would be the very thing that gave you hell

what gave to you

stole from you

what made you feel whole

broke you in half soon after

what spoke love to you

dared to speak lies with the same mouth

- *irony*

if i submerge myself in these words

and somehow drown

at least solitude will fill

my lungs

i admired

souls that moved gracefully

synchronized

like the trees with the wind

and the hymns of the birds

at sunrise

togetherness, perhaps i craved

but dysfunction took place

in our not so sacred sanctuary

because our souls were headed

to different destinations

speak to me

like you know your words

mean something

speak to me

like you know your words

can heal

speak to me

like you know your words

will match the light begging

to illuminate within me

with fear, doubt and worry

as crutches

i'm still not getting anywhere

they get me somewhere

not where i want to be

but somewhere.

i stare at myself

when she is sad and

make room for conversation

with hopes that

maybe healing will finally

make its appearance

one of these days.

we need these talks

maybe i am not that

i could be the opposite

of what you wish me to be

is it even okay if i happen to fail?

what you see is not what i see

i tried to find her

i looked, i searched and still no answer

hidden, i suppose

i can be what you want me to be

but if i cannot, will you view me the same?

i could alter my mind

because i am not as smart, i thought

force intelligence onto me

shove confidence and-

but who am i pleasing?

- *afraid of pedestals*

you carelessly picked my petals

threw them down

stomped on them

tried to pick up and place them back

together again

like the bandages you placed on my stab wounds

only to discover

they had withered

turned brown

and even cracked to reveal

the parts of me left

unattended

my mouth is deceiving

but my eyes

never tell lies

and i cannot apologize if

you see something in them

that chokes you up

or

changes your perception

of what you thought i was

when you didn't know me

- *conviction*

was it my voice

or the hair gifted from my scalp

with more personality than you

was it the fire in my eyes that

beat odds and broke chains

that scared you

was it my walk

that screamed so loudly of

resistance and independence and opulence

that you could not sit still enough to hear

your ego

or maybe

it was my grandmother's prayers

that steered you away

from me

    -   *imbalance // thank you*

voices of deception

and false prophesy

could not get enough of my pure ears

anticipated the contamination of

my psyche

used me until i was no more

obsolete.

stretched me out from here

to there

until there was less of me

and silently rejoiced

at my demise

i watered you
until you grew

you watered me
until i drowned

the craziest thing of it all is
you watched.
no life vest
no rescue team
nothing.

we are not the same

i tried to change
into what i thought was better
i spoke more
i laughed more
i trusted more
i engaged more
only to appeal more

but what good was it
to return home
after the act
after the curtains closed
no standing ovation
and there i was
drained
from being someone
i did not know

- *introverted*

never again

but that was said last time

and the time prior

but this time

i looked in your eyes

and what i saw brought fear

because even then i knew

you knew

this would not be the last

-   *never ending*

please, my heart
stop letting everyone in to
see the depths of you
not ready to be seen
stop with the fragility
you are louder than
need be

i don't know how much longer
i can keep you
together

avoiding human contact

as often

as much as possible

not because i loathe connection

but simply because i never know

what they may think

what they may say

if my words will flow correctly or

will the current take us out completely

if i will make sense at all or

just add confusion

wishing i could be

'the rose that grew from concrete'

i tried to force it

as the final page approached

holding tightly

to the thorns of your stem

bruises, cuts on my hands

that you failed to notice but

i'm sure you did

as you wandered off

to another's

blank pages

i have learned

it is not okay to

be connected

or to crave

connection

connections fail

they can break and

signals weaken and

someone can connect themselves

to me

like a socket

take the power they need

and leave me empty

and dead

i take trips here

involuntarily

mostly at night or

mornings that resemble night

sometimes reflection is haunting

-   *today's hurt*

i am a museum. home of valuable art. constantly misunderstood without remorse and misinterpreted carelessly. only the Creator knows exactly what the art speaks, what it is worth, yet those watching with bare eyes see no such thing. unaware. souls stare and ponder, gather up conclusions that do not reflect its true value or what it even is. purely cutting its price in half, in thirds, then fourths and never getting the story right.

being a work of art comes with a price.

diluted, not by choice.

can i cross your mind and dance a little

careful, yet mesmerizing steps

you could never keep up and i never minded

the music, your heartbeat

my favorite song

you could join me if i wasn't overbearing

but can i cross your mind in child form

innocent and cute

hard to say no to

you, my candy shop

but too much of anything is never good

because now what made my eyes glisten

churns my stomach

not like the butterflies from the beginning

i've had more than i could bear, i welcome the cavity

or can i cross your mind just as a smile

32 teeth

in true form, contagious

because now you're smiling and can't help it

like how the sun can't help but to rise

but with the rise comes the setting and

i'm not sure if i'm ready

but if the sun is set, it will surely rise tomorrow

but

i don't know if i'll make it through the night

or if we'll make it through the night

but tomorrow isn't promised

our tomorrow isn't promised

- *costs and benefits*

47

i wanted you to hurt

as bad as i did

rip your heart from your chest

ask you how it feels

break you apart

piece by piece with

you under my fingernails

with sorrow and defeat in your eyes

i will look down at you

and say

sorry

i apologize

- *switch*

i craft for consumption

and feed you these words by spoon

sour, bitter and sweet

but i hope you don't mind

i give you permission to spit them out

just as i did on this paper

because not even i can fathom the taste

more like vinegar than maple, so i blame none

i've always been a picky eater

but i was not allowed to pick at this diner

of my mind, heart and soul

i'm sorry it's not your favorite meal

allow me to offer substitutions instead

as i did when i dipped and buried my pens

in fear

and picked at the scabs of my misfortunes

i'm still trying to acquaint myself with the taste

   -   *because everything isn't sweet here*

if i loved

i was weak

if i trusted

i was dumb

if i demanded

i was controlling

if i was assertive

i was intimidating

if i questioned

i was simply tripping

- *a woman*

you are truly one of a kind

the space between us is cold, chilling

and worthy of teeth clenching

do not stir up a combustion of movement between

you and i

with unclear intentions just for everything

to come to a halt soon after.

i am as fragile as my heart

and the emotions i tuck under my skin.

to dream dreams that did not

believe in the nightmares lived

of reality

awakened covered in petals

of sorrow

that lingered from passions

stunk of let-downs

past and present

left to grieve alone for

the things killed not by me

i wipe my eyes until

they hurt and sting like

my heart when the scent of others

consumes you to the point where

i'm nauseous

you evaded.

just as my rest

when i question if the worth

of myself

matches the blood on my hands

from protecting you

and scars of the voices left on me

that tell me what

i not want but

need to hear

if only i wore love

as well as i wore pain

- *hopeful*

winning battles, yet

losing wars

as i feel stuck in my own space

one moment i am okay

then there you are

crawling back in

with devil eyes

and an evil grin

ready to take hold of me

to remind me

i am not okay after all

but i was able to defeat you

only after realizing

i was never healed

i was distracted

- *depression*

i vomit poems and prose from my body

whenever i digest something

with a bad taste

that carries sicknesses

that my body nor spirit agree with and

wishes it was unfamiliar

because it is better to have it all

laid out on these sheets of paper

than to have it on my chest

than to keep forcing it down and

dealing with the taste

because if i taste it

others will

for if i do not release it

it will eventually transform into a

parasite

and reflect on me

-   *learning to cope*

i allowed people, things even, to taunt me. i had to be let down so i could learn to pick myself up. i needed to learn to trust myself. the toxic mindset, relationships and the heartbreaks that accompanied them may have ignited this fire, but it lit the way for my other demons i refused to acknowledge. that is when i saw my mistake. i claimed them. i unknowingly danced with the devil until my feet bled.

i could not have bloomed with bad soil. i had to learn this was not only about what others had done to me but more of what i had done to myself. what i settled for. what i allowed to roam freely in my aura. what i chose to tolerate. the lies i told myself. the thoughts i entertained. the damage i put my mind, body and spirit through. the cycles of self-hatred i became oblivious to. i had become my enemy.

it was time for me to break away from my old self, so i could make myself available to welcome my blossoming.

the pruning

new pens

new pages

for softer stories

note to self:

listen to me.

there is nothing wrong with you.

there is something about the woman i am

that leaves a tattoo of my name

on your wrist where it hurts

you will forget me but

with each glance at yourself

the memories of me will

ambush you.

even when i am gone

there i am

i will listen to my hurt

and my pain and even the tears

that fall without notice

i'll entertain and release

before it kills the me i haven't

gotten to know yet

but they cannot make a home out

of me

they cannot stay here

to torment and control

like there's hell on earth

i cannot allow it

they have to go.

for the first time

in a long time

i breathed for myself, by myself

i exhaled the burdens of others

and inhaled the aroma of life

and stillness

removing deception from my chest

and the voices of ghosts i once ate with

i became lighter enough to

grace the atmospheres where

i am needed

what i needed

could not be rushed

or else

authenticity would be lost

every flower

has its season

to bloom

-   *patience*

pray for people

and keep it moving

you do not have to keep in touch

or feel obligated

to save them

everyone cannot be saved

- *nina*

note to self:

it is not my obligation

to put anything back

together

that i did not rip apart

i deserve a great love

a love

with eyes for me

a love

that does not creep

i deserve a great love

one that will bring

more smiles than tears

more security

than uncertainty

i deserve a great love

that respects my independency

that is not frightened

by my growth

surely, i deserve a great love

but if no one delivers

i will give myself

a great love

love does not hate us. do you really think our Creator would gift us anything intended to bring harm? love does not hate you. we were hurt by people who do not know how to love because they were never shown love. we do not have a problem with love, the problem is with those who offered false interpretations of what love is.

love does not lie. love does not steal. love does not bring agony. people do.

if you allow a cloud

to stick around too long

it will darken

become full

release its rain

and gradually

stump your growth

i have no offspring

no child has left my womb

do not expect the things of a child from me

do not expect to be raised by me

who said i was your mother?

- *we asked for partners, not sons*

i want love that makes

me softer and

soothes the rough parts

left by those before

but accepts them

at the same time

works with me like

a craftsman but without intent

to fix me

like a project

engaging in conversation to express my feelings does not scream *i am angry*. it whispers softly and sweetly, *please, listen to me.* everyone wants to be heard, but no one is willing to listen. no one wants to learn how to listen. vulnerability takes courage. it is not an easy task for me to take on. for me to be willing to do such means more than you think. it takes courage to speak these things and to open my hidden pages for you, even when i hate it, and you stole that from me. the next time, you will probably wonder why i don't tell you things. why i don't open up to you as i should. as i wish i could. why are my emotions written in pages you would never read, kept in boxes that move everywhere i move. dragged in a way. well, the answers are right there.

- *to everyone*

i shifted my focus
shifted my thoughts
so that they may heal me
and not break me
anymore

i shifted along with the atmosphere
i was determined to create
for myself, by myself

selfish,

i will be

because you return

after you realized

what you chased is not what you thought it was

so here you are asking me

to help you

to pray for you

but i am selfish now

my guardian angel smiles

i will not give you time, energy nor satisfaction

a flower with a newly strengthened stem

cannot be forsaken like before

with your tricks and games

you made your bed

now, lie in it

as they say

you cannot neglect yourself,

your health or

your feelings that beg for your

attention while

trying to fix another's

self

inflicted

problems

my God created unique wonders

with the brush of purpose in His hand

He took his time perfecting

each and every masterpiece

slowly crafting every single detail

most will not even get to see

or experience

half, a third of what lies beyond

and in all of that

He still thought to create you, too

do you still think you are any less

than unique

or that everyone is deserving

to experience you, too?

- *i am a wonder*

i am not the seeds of dandelions

that you can pick and blow

and witness them move carelessly in the wind

for your amusement

grab a game

because i am not it

you cannot pray for signs

then once God delivers

and those signs make their appearance

you look

the other way

they will return

to your face

but louder

we look at others

and point out what they did to us

but what if we looked at ourselves

and focused on

what we allowed others to do to us

and why we felt it was okay

to suffer under the hands of another human

now i know

i can close doors

and build a gated community

with these hands

when people do not love themselves, they will paint
false narratives to make themselves feel better. this
is a mixture of pride, guilt and shame. they will
twist unfortunate stories that you lived through and
victimize themselves, meanwhile the harm was
actually done at their hands. when someone is
twisting the minds of others who do not know them
in order to paint a better picture of themselves, let
them. the truth will always surface. you do not need
to prove to anyone you were the one who was
wounded while the suspect is spreading falsehood.
you are not a victim anymore. save your energy for
those goals of yours. just remember, no tongue that
rises in the name of lies against you will rise
forever. let them talk, let them manipulate others.
live in your freedom from those hands. i hope you
can look past things of such and get the rest you've
deserved for a long time. sleep soundly.

- *power*

i traded my pain

for words

my cries

for meditating

my fears

for trust

my doubts

for hope

and my worries

for strength

- *exchange*

do not confuse genuine check ups

with someone who is just checking

on your availability

to help occupy

the dark hole they created

by themselves

- *i'm doing fine, declined*

one day

my eyes will tell stories

that my voice cannot support

stare into them, get lost in them

and you will see the things

not spoken of

never acknowledged

for my voice would shake and stutter

but my eyes

will do them justice

- *eyes tell no lies*

get to know me, first

and maybe one day

i'll brew tea and

hope it isn't too hot for you

then we can sit in communion

and put light on

your poorly arranged pre-judgments

of me

- *but i'll probably be busy*

i no longer crave flowers

desperately

from hearts i do not know

or hearts i used to know

because i have mirrors now

mirrors that love me and i love them

mirrors that make me sing

and feel

i am exotic, i am all the flowers

the flowers you never had

they put themselves first

you put yourself last

if it were reversed

they would make sure you knew

                           - *choose yourself*

the ideal me ten years from now radiates love. love for those who need it and love for those who are undeserving. those are the ones who need it the most. i want to be a reflection of the greatest love. when you speak to me i want you to feel loved and i hope my words touch you in the places that need them. i hope my love brings the right amount of light to your dark spots. when you look at me i hope you will see love. i hope i am viewed like your favorite meal after fasting or your favorite show that puts you through emotional trauma, but you love it, so you keep watching it. i want to show those broken that everyone is not here to break you. i will not break you. i believe i was put back together to help others be put back together but only with love. i want to love a little more. hatred has taken over but i am still convinced love holds power like none other.

- *nonverbal*

my light

will not dim

to please

it will not dim

to reflect its surroundings

it will not dim

for the likes of others

it will not dim

to make you comfortable

it

will

not

dim

-    *unapologetic*

loving someone
is not conditional on
keeping them around

reciprocation.

give to me and i will give to you. i am not capable
of giving more than what is received. equality does
not have its limits. me planting the seeds of yours
while you weaken the roots of mine is not ideal and
will not be romanticized.

we cannot ask for what we cannot offer. we cannot
give to others what we fail to give to ourselves.

do not neglect

the areas of you that have wilted

those parts make your story

those parts

put value on

your blossoming

nourish them

- *care for them*

note to self:

stop offering discounts

as if you were

generic

you are expensive, act like it

someone who loves you

will make it known

you will not have to

beg

nag

scream

or compromise with

how you should

how you deserve

to be loved

you deserve more than a sorry

from someone who knew

the effects of their actions

before they acted

you can do all the right things

be a listening ear

be a blanket of comfort

be the medicine to their troubles

feed them without food

send prayers left and right

bleed loyalty

and trust

but if someone

does not want to love you

they will not love you

if someone is still blind to your

value

it was by choice

        -   *hard pills*

it is a disservice to yourself

to repeatedly allow

the people

the thoughts

the habits

of chaos

and self-destruction

to re-enter your garden

whenever they see fit

- *serpents*

it does not make you a bad person

to realize when

you must love someone

from a distance

it makes you a smart person

because so many do not learn that

until it is too late

and they are stuck in the hole

with the person

that created it

- *tony*

freedom reigned

the minute those doors closed

the doors i desperately tried

to keep open

not to self:

this walk i am taking

is not a race

there is no competition

even if i must

walk alone

i will persevere

i always persevere

note to self:

thank your failures. thank your setbacks. embrace
them. without them, you would not know what it
took to win. your time will come, that is inevitable.
your success is waiting.

we want others to be

our peace

but true, genuine peace starts with

self.

relying on others

and giving them that much power, that executive
position

of a peace source

is a setup

when that soul departs from you

is your peace gone?

girl, get up. do your laundry. you have been wearing the same garments of hurt, fear, betrayal, doubt, worry and unforgiveness for way too long. these heavy clothes, soiled with regret, are keeping you from moving, from elevating, from living freely and being the woman you were created to be. do not get too comfortable harboring clothes filthy and reeking of the burdens of insecurities and problems of the circumstances of your physical being. you cannot cultivate in these clothes. your spiritual being is assuring you there is no room for this and these clothes need to be washed.

- *for my sisters*

being in my own company is not an invitation for comfort from outside sources. i am not okay with anyone feeling entitled to steal my peace. the boundaries i have set for myself would not allow such sorcery. unheard of.

letting go

was up to me

for me

to save myself

for once i was first

and you,

you could not stand it

- *oh well*

the only person
i am obligated to be
or do anything for
is me

i am entitled to me

you need tender loving care

just as your garden does

because gardeners cannot tend

to their creations

and treasures

rooting from the ground up

without rest, energy or love

- *recharge when needed*

i am being put back together again. the process is heart-aching, frustrating, but beautiful. i am letting go. sometimes i crave stagnation just to avoid facing and learning how strong i really am. i am not perfect, yet i am improving. that is what i love about this journey, this walk. i am nowhere i aspire to be but am beyond grateful i am not where i was. i am not who i was. thank God.

the blooming

showing up on time

for all the things missed and

every good thing with my name

written on it

for everything taken from me

without warning

i received abundantly more than

what was ever lost

miss my harvesting

just as

you missed my planting

do not expect to reap

what you did not sow

look at me

in love with myself

after i thought i could never

love anyone else

the way i loved you

i appreciate how i can take words

and gestures

created to hurt and discredit me

and make bouquets of them to

gift to the mouths

they left

you need to believe in you.

you need to trust you.

you need you.

the love of myself

embraced me like silk, smooth to the touch

caressed my body perfectly

like a long-awaited hug from a long-lost friend

this one did not hurt

i was made aware it was here to stay

permanently, no fear of negligence followed

i wept at its arrival, unbelievable to my own
understanding

was it meant to feel this good

my only wish

is that others will experience this love, too

- *true love*

i'm sorry

the love and peace

and security

that invaded my soul

stole your place and

there's no room for you anymore

                              -   *to my insecurities*

i accepted a relationship

with discernment

so that i know when

something is for me

and when

something is against me

i no longer fear the answer

i no longer fear things that support me

your peace

your heart

your mind

your craft

your energy

your joy

your time

your space

your passions

you.

- *things that must be protected*

blooming showed me my flaws, but in a loving way that was free from judgment and open to maturation. the process opens the doors of reflection and sheds light on what needs to be corrected. blooming shows us it isn't okay to stare out of windows longing for happiness we are unknowingly preventing. i have discernment and can recognize when i am subjecting myself to things that don't support the level of happiness i aspire to. it is okay to let go of things that don't measure up with my potential. my heart no longer drops at the thought of letting go, moving forward and not caring what no tongue dare rises to say.

i unraveled like a rose at spring

except i didn't have to wait until spring

my petals unfolded so gracefully, so

unexpectedly

heads turned, eyes widened

smiles rushed to the faces of my seeds

serenity exhausted itself upon me

like the morning breeze that brushed my cheeks

and greeted my hair

as i stepped into my destiny

surrounded by gardens unnoticed before

my peripheral expanded

as i indulged and gulped at the newfound sight

i almost didn't recognize me

this had become me

- *becoming*

my blossoming scared people away
who no longer served a purpose in my life

i waved as they left

my closed doors of wilting

led me to open,

more welcoming

doors of blooming

like flowers in the spring time

and my browns, blacks and greys

turned to vibrant, lively

greens and yellows

the power of words saved me

therapy.

i entered and sat

told my story, my pains

and we kind of reached

common ground.

and they listened

anxiety vacated my body

because for once i spoke without interruption

forced to listen

held me in a way that

was unfamiliar to me

and prescribed to me

what i already knew

- *antidote*

i planted seeds of honesty

and glorious, awaited resiliency

upon my skin

to cover and heal

the lies once spoken to me

so that i could fully embrace

and welcome my blossoming

with arms ready to hold onto

without ceasing

never block your blessings
in attempts to reciprocate
bad energy

resilient.

because no emotion became stronger

than you

because you crafted solitude where it was never

meant to exist

because you wiped tears so a smile could take

their place

because even when storms knocked you off

your feet

you stood up after

here i am removing weeds

bent at my knees, wiping sweat

with my forearm

removing what should not be here

cleansing my garden

so that my children and

their children can grow

abundantly

without the hardships of my own

-   *breaking generational curses*

i leave my petals behind in rooms

you will know of my presence
wherever
you
go.

- *impact*

where did you learn this behavior

to bite your tongue

until it bled

as an attempt to prevent

the flow of life

to restrict your creative

to step out of sight and be

the shadow of others

who said

you belong back there

when you were created

to be out front

i knew it was over for them

once i crafted comfort

out of loneliness

brew herbs

wash your face

and remove the tear stains

and impurities

of what used to be

now feel your face

it is softer

just as you became when

you removed the bits planted

in you

that made you hard

for everything i thought i lost

there was a gain waiting

so i no longer fear losing

whenever i feel myself

drifting back into the

sorrows of regret

i am reminded that whatever leaves me

is making room for

better.

i needed to go on dates

with myself

quality time.

to figure me out

to learn what it takes to win me over

and cause my hands to willingly

without force

helplessly unite with another's

clasped tightly like they hold my future

to learn what it looks like

to love myself

and to discover what

song my heart sings when greeted by

love

so that i can now discern

when a soul different from mine

is offering love

or uncertainty

i took the dark places

that were home to my oppositions

and blames

that kept me trapped in my temple

gave them support and

guided them

to reach higher callings

and turned them into fertilizer

now i catch myself staring

and stargazing at

my skin

my shape and

everything within

from my nose

to my toes

from bone to bone

and everything i've missed before

neglected and ignored because i

kept myself

occupied by everything else

i've truly missed out

-   *i am in love*

if you feel

you are undeserving

of anything great,

greater than you

go after it

reach for it

claim it

you deserve it

i can live a joyous, fulfilled life

even if my soul

or hands

are not joined with another's

i am learning to love my company

you quilted pieces of healing

out of brokenness

with hands made of gold and

ambition

in efforts to support the flowers

pushed from between your legs

you passed this quilt down to them

knowing the inevitable

patch after patch knitted

with purpose beyond what eyes could see

and what mouths could speak

how ironic is it that

the words spoken to

bring you down and

place road blocks in your journey

became the very words

used as stools

that lifted you higher

and wrote your name on

blessings

to hurt, to feel pain

is inevitable

but to rejoice and claim a healing

that the eye cannot see

is a choice

i am a museum

home of valuable art with

prices set by the Creator that

cannot be negotiated

a furrow for me, my sister

and women of other wombs

a place of solitude like the one ached for

in prayers

skins turned as radiant as the sun

areas forgotten gently confronted

the home of prayers for prosperity,

healing and wholeness

strength and backbone

spoken by the gardener without condemnation, no
rejection

every serpent casted out

a place like no other of plants

and mending hearts that began

blooming without notice

resuscitated.

with words missed and words foreign, but desired

- *my mother's garden*

145

note to self:

healing looks good on you

peace looks good on you

you look good on you

the mission has been assigned to

honor myself

nothing less and anything that was

does not measure up to who i am

they always fall short.

celebratory dinners are thrown in my honor

in the name of resiliency

a toast is announced

for the name that trembles the violins

yawning in your chest, my name

that grew anchors of stillness to

keep me rooted

where need be until my purpose

is driven.

note to self:

i hope you reach the point where your time to blossom is not reliant upon the physical season or even your circumstances of now. you are strong enough to bloom in winter, whatever winter may be for you. every season is your opportunity to bloom. make every season yours. you have the tools.

one day

i will have a seat

with the chest of the segments

of my old self

that needed to be stripped from me

i will sit with them

face to face

and comfort them

like the new clothes on my back

i look at myself not how i used to

there are cultivated curves

magnificent layers

pristine color

a captivating fragrance

and abundant growth

i will tell my daughter

contrary to what we are taught

you must be picky

pick wisely and cautiously

when choosing spirits to give your time to

be picky

when choosing what you let enter

the gates of your garden

pick carefully what battles

you take on

be picky because

not everything, nor everyone

deserves to experience

you

- *be picky*

i am the result of the prayers

of women before me

i had no choice but to bloom

i will continue to grow

even against grimy weather

my journey was not and will not be perfect

but i will gather up any wilted flowers

along the way

a bouquet pleases the eye more than a single flower

it is stronger

and more aesthetically pleasing

than a single rose

- *empathy*

a vision

a dream

a thought

a gift

none were placed in you

for you to sleep on

- *woke*

it is okay to believe

you are worthy of more

than what they

make it seem

than what you have

led yourself

to believe

i am thankful for evolving

and being able to create when

creativity seems to be on vacation

i take pieces of encouragement

and kind words

thrown carefully, gracefully at me

and sew them into blankets, scarves

and coats

to wear when the weather becomes cruel, cold

and unforgiving

as a reminder that

i have everything i need to get past

this

who i am today

will not compare

to who i will be tomorrow

- *be afraid*

i love you, but you cannot come with me. i dragged you as long as i could, but my strength was depleting. i was never supposed to carry more than myself.

i care for you, but you are not allowed here.

i can help you but if helping you means losing myself i have to pass.

you matter, but i matter more this time.

this is what self-love looks like.

these days

i find value and delight in what is overlooked

thrown to the side and mistaken

as something less than

it's the littlest things that tell the best stories

the most self-hating thing

i had done to myself

was to deny my feelings

my feelings of hurt, jealousy and anger

it took time

almost a decade, or a century

for me to learn

it is okay to feel

with each day i am gifted

i will wake and ponder what it is

i can do

to care for me a little more

to love me a little harder

to infect those nearby with the plague of 'finding'

because i'm finding myself, too

i discovered how
to create comfort where
it did not live

i found joy
without staring
in another's eyes

i pieced and mixed and
did whatever i could
night and day
to figure out what
had no formula

i cultivated me.

i have a garden to cultivate

a multitude of

art

beauty

visions

and crafts

that need to be cared for

nurtured.

and pests are not welcomed

-

you cannot attend

my blossoming

when you were absent

during my wilting

there's something strange
yet beautiful
conjuring between my peace
and joy
they met one another and became
inseparable.
i danced down the hall and witnessed
security and love conversing in awe within
these walls
catching up
over the time missed between the two
after longing for each other as i longed for
me
my tea is not the only thing
brewing in my home

unlike my favorite fruits

i am always in season

i am comfort

i am the warm home that you walk into

after pushing through a day

of sleet and snow

the aroma of warm vanilla

that taps your nose

i am the glass of water

after running miles in search of

understanding

i am the spark

at a campfire that resembles my eyes

did you really think i would bring the spirit of wilt
to my garden?

the garden i cultivated

with my bare hands

my crown, an umbrella

pushed through storms of destruction and
distraction

created to prolong my harvesting

to plant what i needed

to love, again

to live, again

to survive

this is not a home for old things

i am awakened each morning
by the welcoming, loving voices
of my petals
that remind me
the world needs to see you today

she walked on the runway of
dignity
with her head to the skies
as high as her sun
that awakened her garden
with a plethora of hope
and skin glowing without the sun's reflection
she left those things behind
that encouraged wilting

i picked up shattered fragments of myself

and built

comfort and love

serenity and contentment

a home.

created from scratch with

stronger foundations of steel

to withstand

when you see me

i am sure

you will confuse me with

petals dancing in the wind

swiftly

carelessly

without a care of who watches

- *freedom*

my flowers made their peak

my season came

fresh, colorful petals

to drive out what

went pale

with the softest, welcoming scent

even after the harshest winter

i rose

i am a rose

- *bloomed*

Made in the USA
San Bernardino, CA
25 June 2020